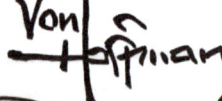

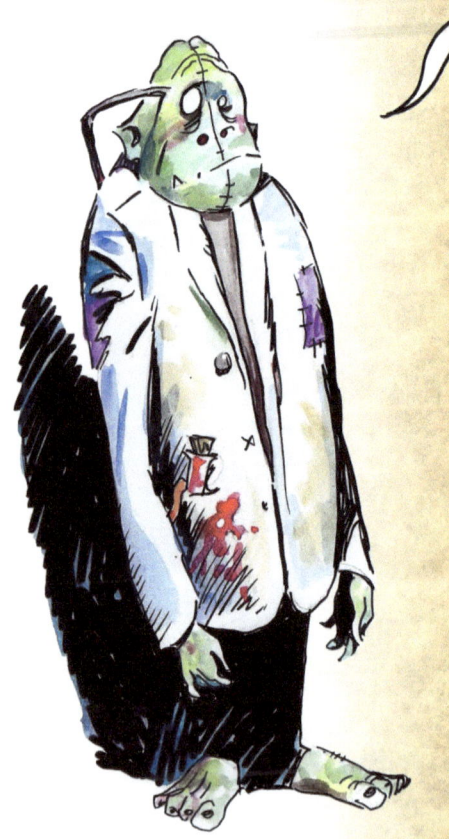

THE SPOOKY HALLOWEEN ART BOOK

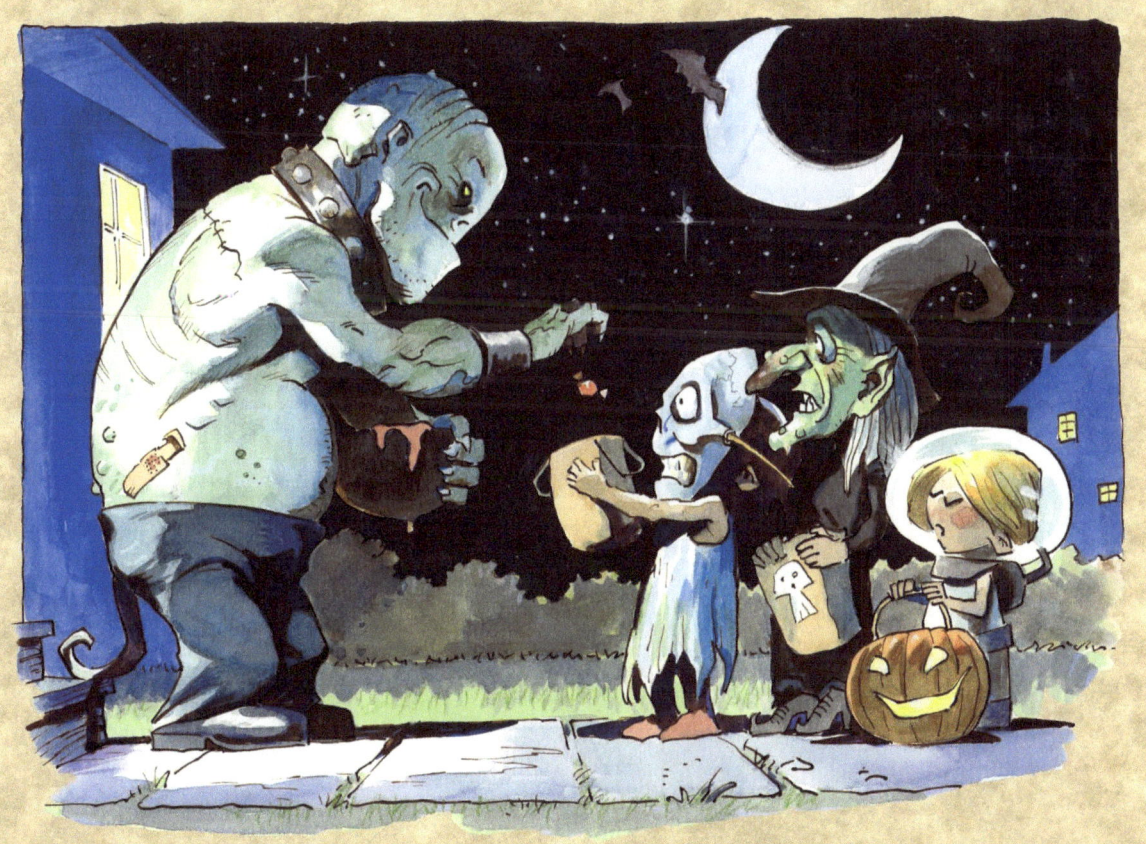

BY MIKE VON HOFFMAN

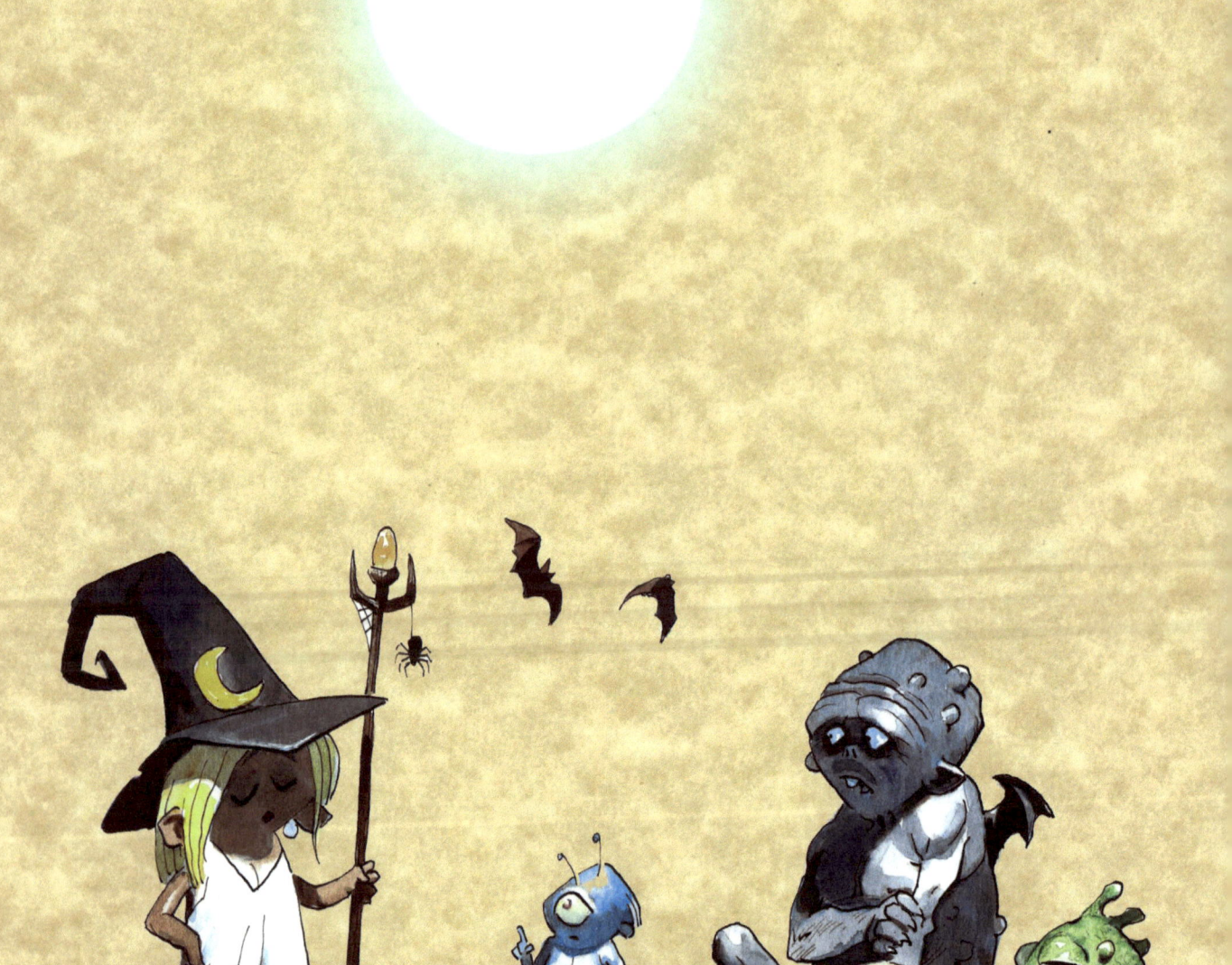

TABLE OF
CONTENTS

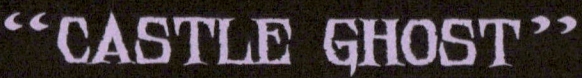

"CASTLE GHOST"

THE SPIRIT OF A
LONG—DEAD LOVER
HAUNTS THIS PLACE
A CASTLE OF STONE
NOW RUINED AND OVERGROWN

SHE WEEPS IN THE DARKNESS
THE BRIDE TO BE
THAT NEVER WAS
ENWRAPPED BY SADNESS
AND A KIND OF MADNESS

A HUNDRED YEARS AGO TODAY
HER GHOST STILL CHOSE
NOT TO PASS ON BY TO STAY
UNTIL HER LOVE FADES AWAY

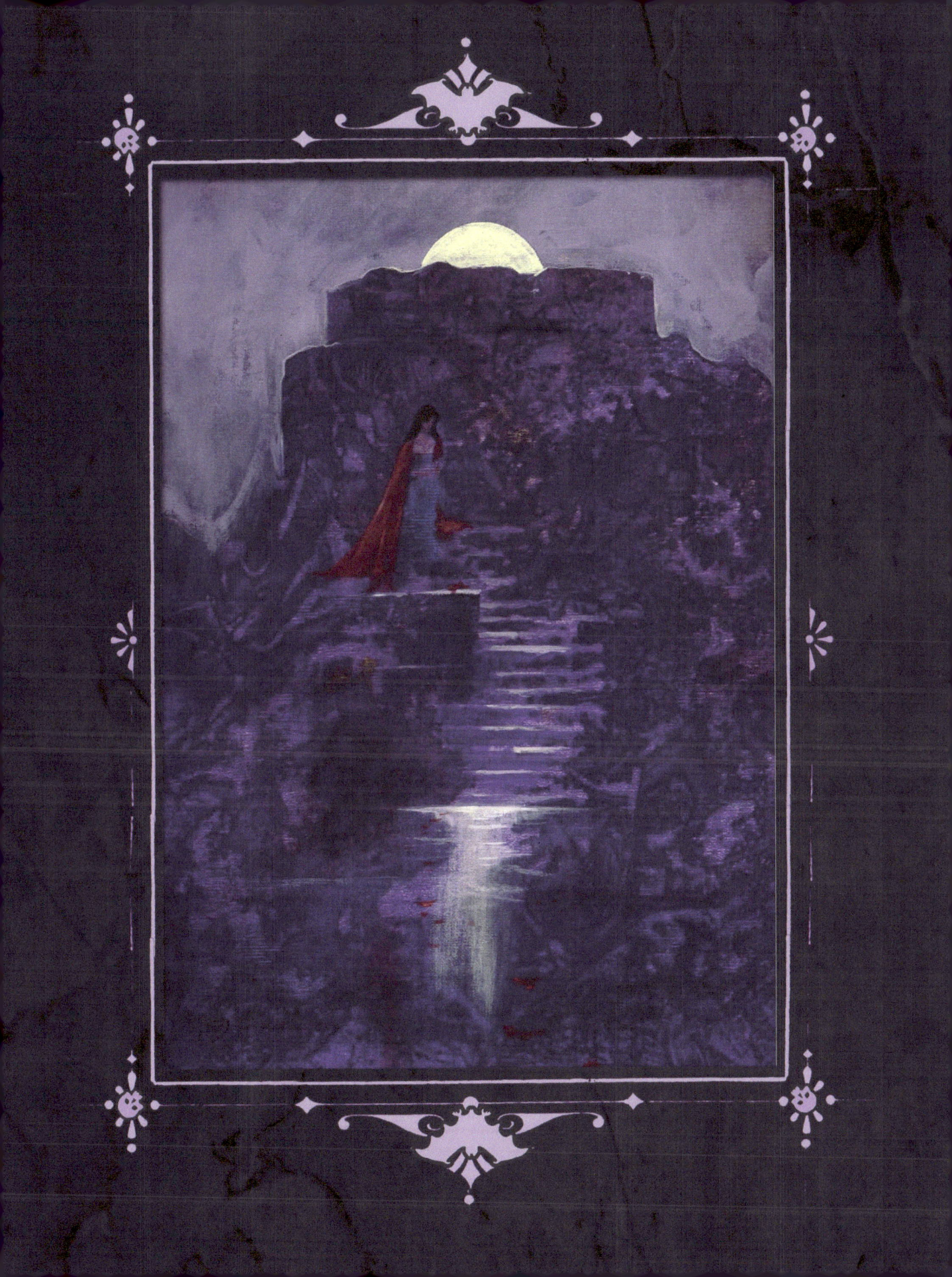

"OCTOBER TREE"

EVERY YEAR
ABOUT THIS TIME
WHEN THE LEAVES TURN
ORANGE, RED AND BROWN
FALLING LIKE SNOW
AND PILING UP ON THE GROUND
MAKING MOUNTAINS FOR CHILDREN
TO FALL INTO LIKE CLOWNS
THE GHOSTS OF HALLOWEENS
PAST, PRESENT AND FUTURE
HANG JACK O' LANTERNS UP
IN THE BRANCHES OF TREES
TO REMIND LITTLE ONES
WHO SEE THEM
WHAT HALLOWEEN
REALLY MEANS

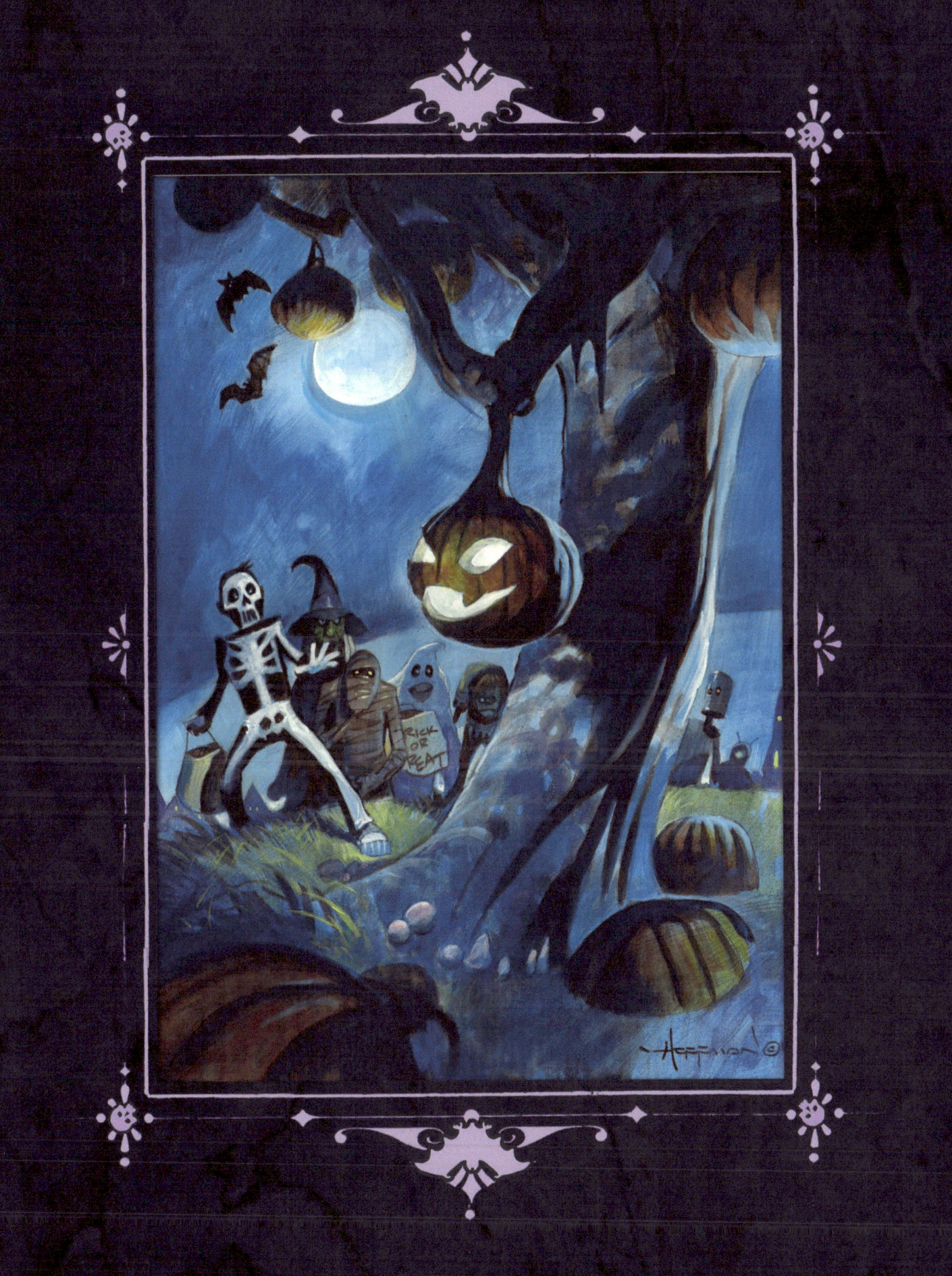

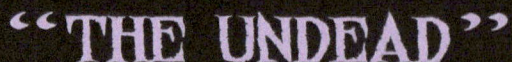

"THE UNDEAD"

WHEN YOU'RE DEAD
YOU KNOW WHO YOUR FRIENDS ARE
WEREWOLVES AND VAMPIRES
THE CHILDREN OF THE NIGHT

WHEN YOU'RE LOST
TO THE WORLD OF THE LIVING
AND ALL OF THEIR FACES
ARE FORGOTTEN AT THE END

THE MOON RISES HIGH
BLACK BATS
SPIN THROUGH THE SKY
AND ALL THE ENDLESS YEARS
PASS YOU BY
WHEN YOU DIE

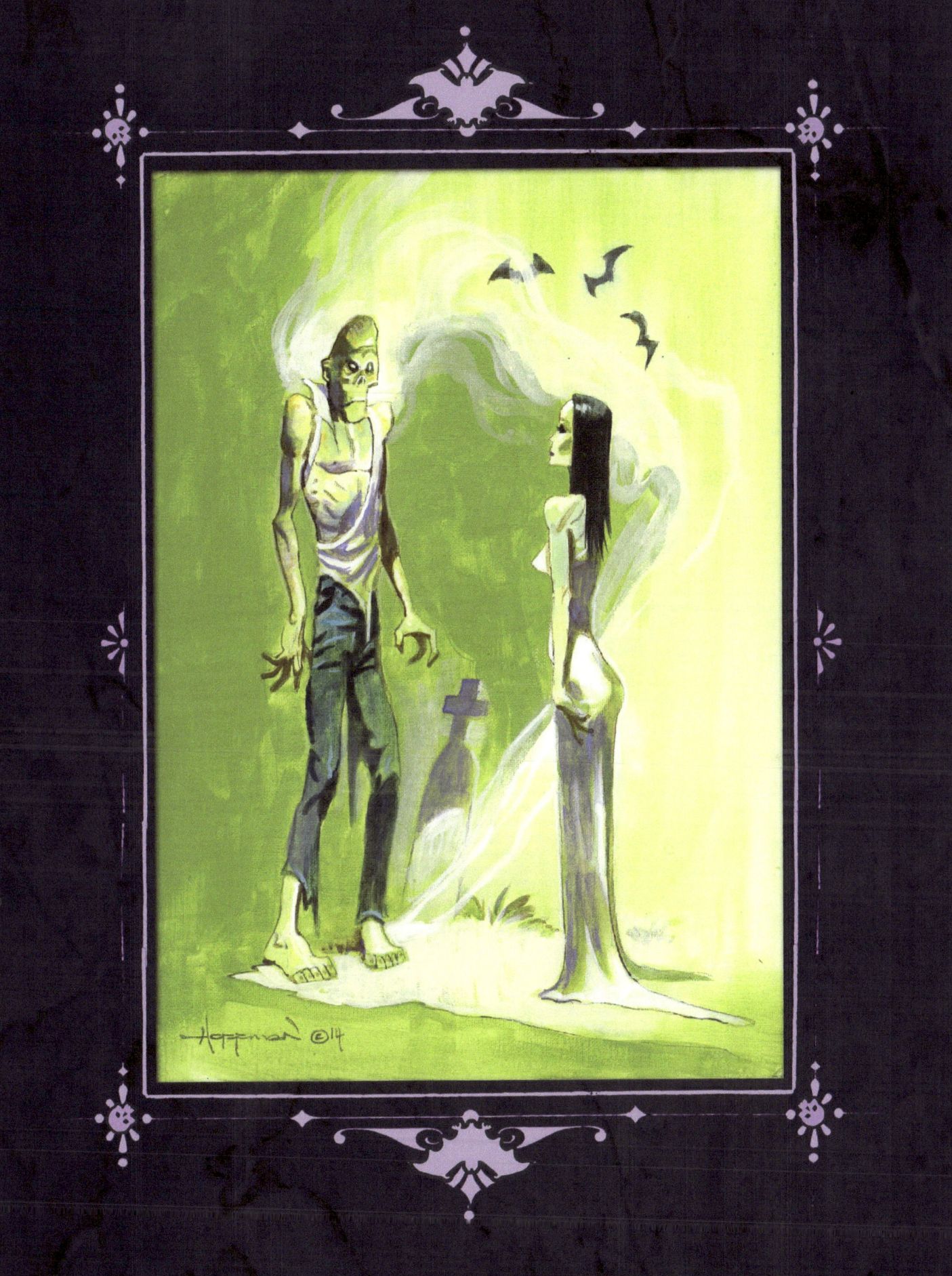

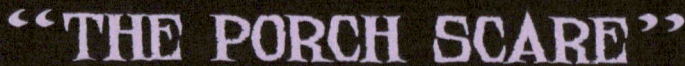

"THE PORCH SCARE"

KNOCK! KNOCK!
KNOCK! KNOCK!
LITTLE FINGERS RAP HARD
ON THE OLD WOODEN DOOR
LEFT SLIGHTLY AJAR...
COURAGE, MEN!
AND SO INTO THE FRAY
THREE COSTUMED MUSKETEERS
ARE NOW QUAKING IN FEAR,
BUT NO ACTING AFRAID
NOTHING TO WORRY FOR
THEY'RE JUST GROWN-UPS
DRESSED UP LIKE WE ARE
BUT WHY ARE THOSE FINGERS
SO ICY COLD?
AND THOSE WERE THE LAST
WORDS THAT THEY SPOKE

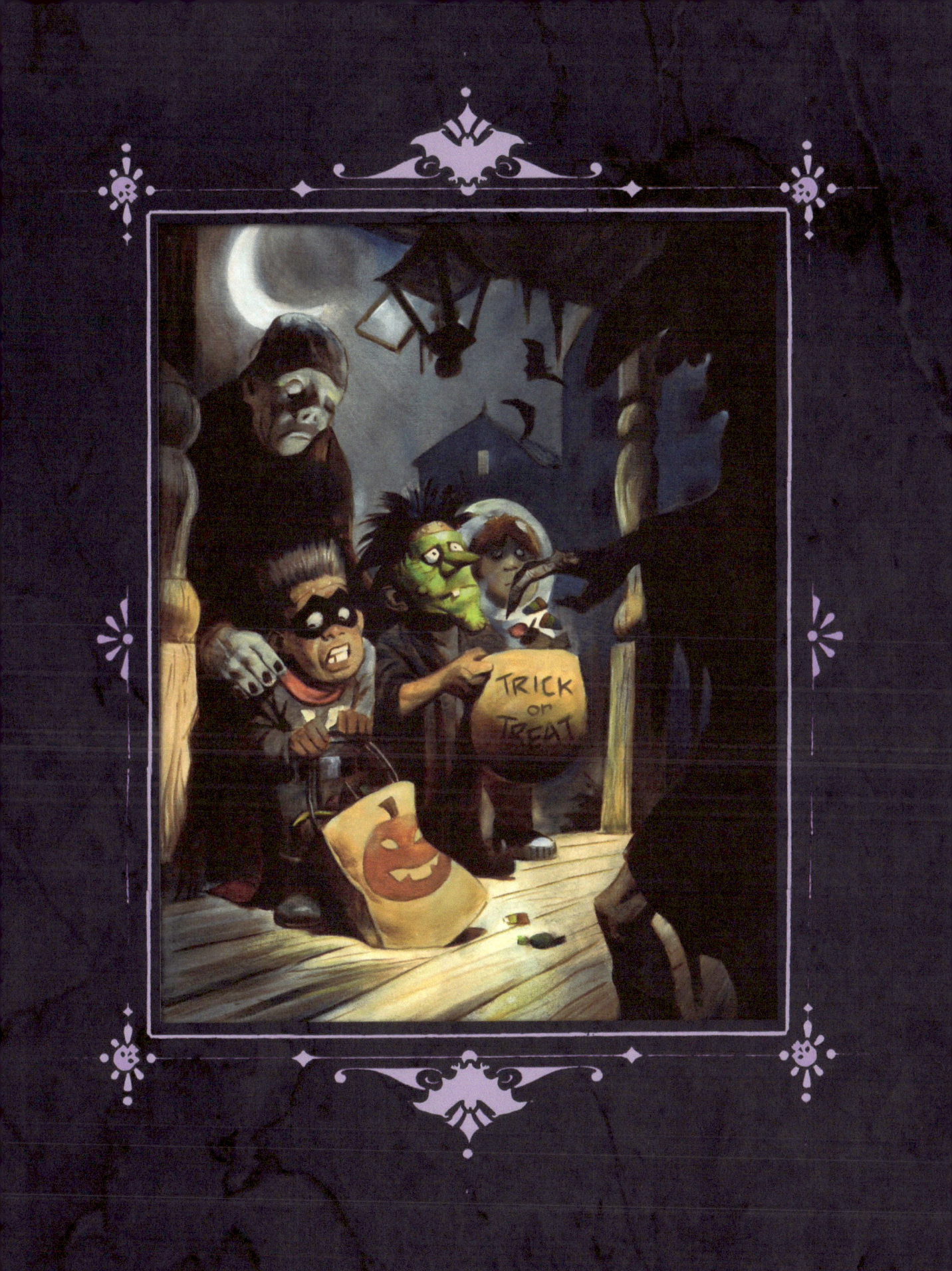

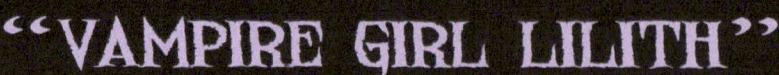

"VAMPIRE GIRL LILITH"

VAMPIRES ARE FOREVER
IN THE BLACKNESS
OF THE NIGHT
HIDING FROM THE LIGHT

THOSE DEAD LIVES
GO ON ETERNALLY
THOUGH WE ARE
LOST TO TIME
WHEN THE YEARS
HAVE ALL GONE BY

IS IT TRUE
WE LIVE AGAIN?

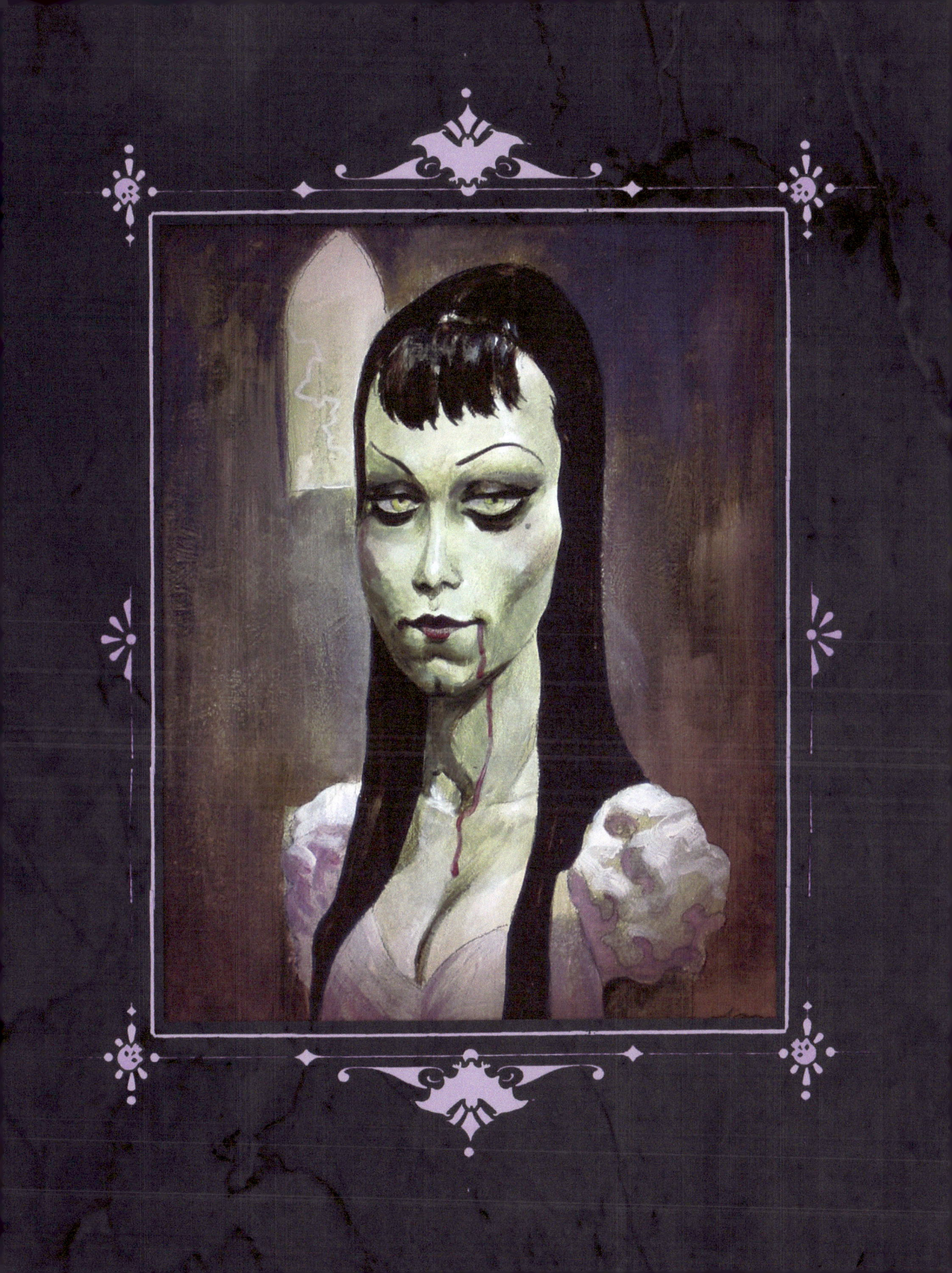

"THE WEREWOLF"

BY DAY
HE'S PRONE TO FIGHT
ONE WHO NEVER PRAYED
BY NIGHT
HE PREYS ON MEN
AND ANY BEAST WHO
CANNOT MATCH
HIS FRIGHTENING BITE

BETWEEN WAX
AND WANE
HE CAN BE SLAIN
IF YOU CARRY
THE WOLF'S BANE

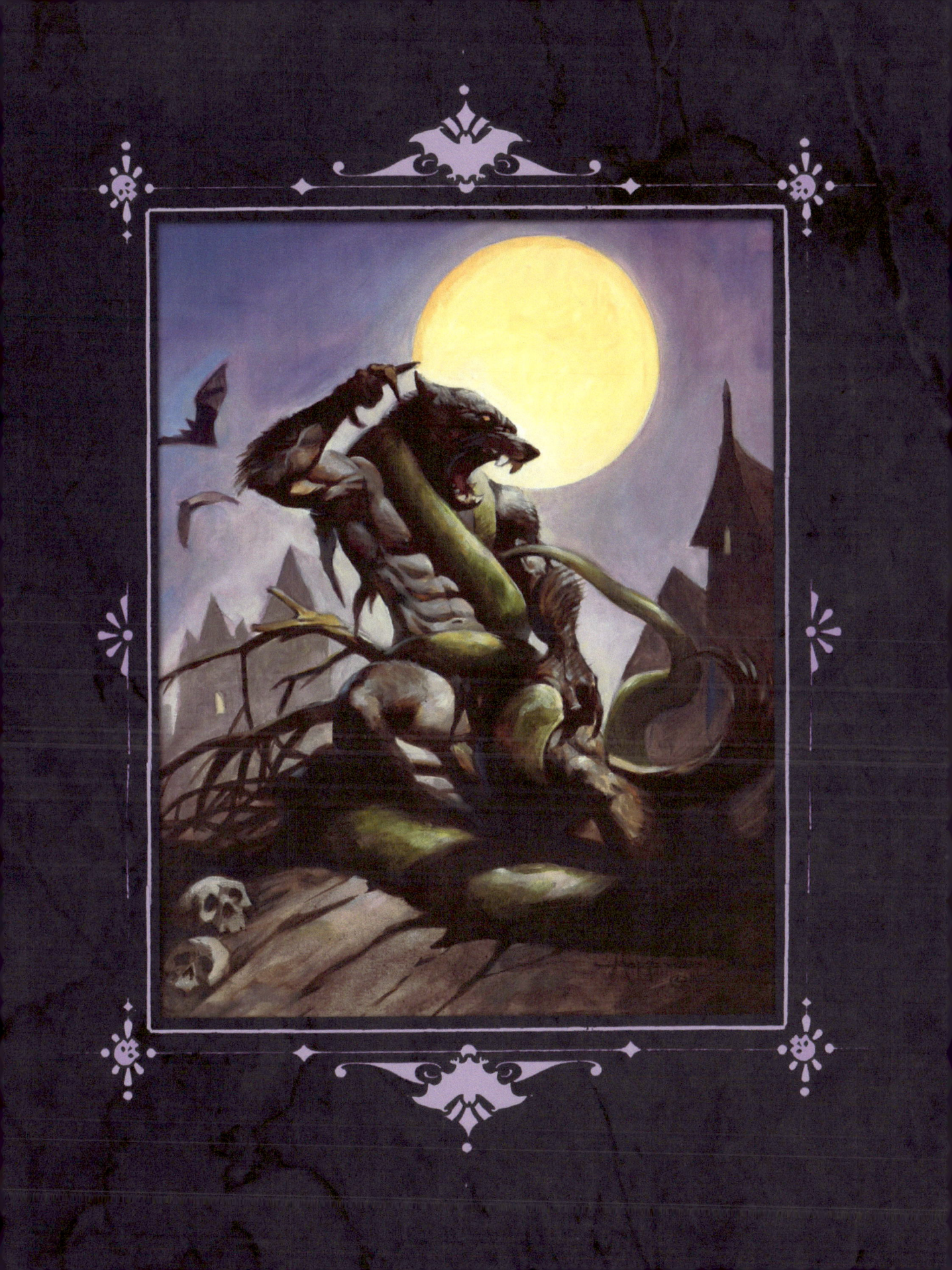

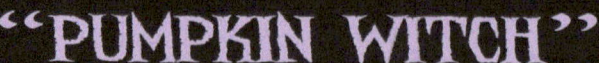

"PUMPKIN WITCH"

LITTLE HILDA WAS NICE
AS WITCHES GO
SHE WENT OFF TO
WITCH SCHOOL
BUT HATED BOILING NEWTS
AND SALAMANDERS
AND STIRRING POTIONS
ALL DAY LONG

SHE DROPPED OUT
OF COLLEGE 'HEX U.'
THEY SAID IT WAS
'A LACK OF AMBITION'
BUT ALL SHE REALLY WANTED
TO DO WAS TO STAY OUT
OF THE KITCHEN

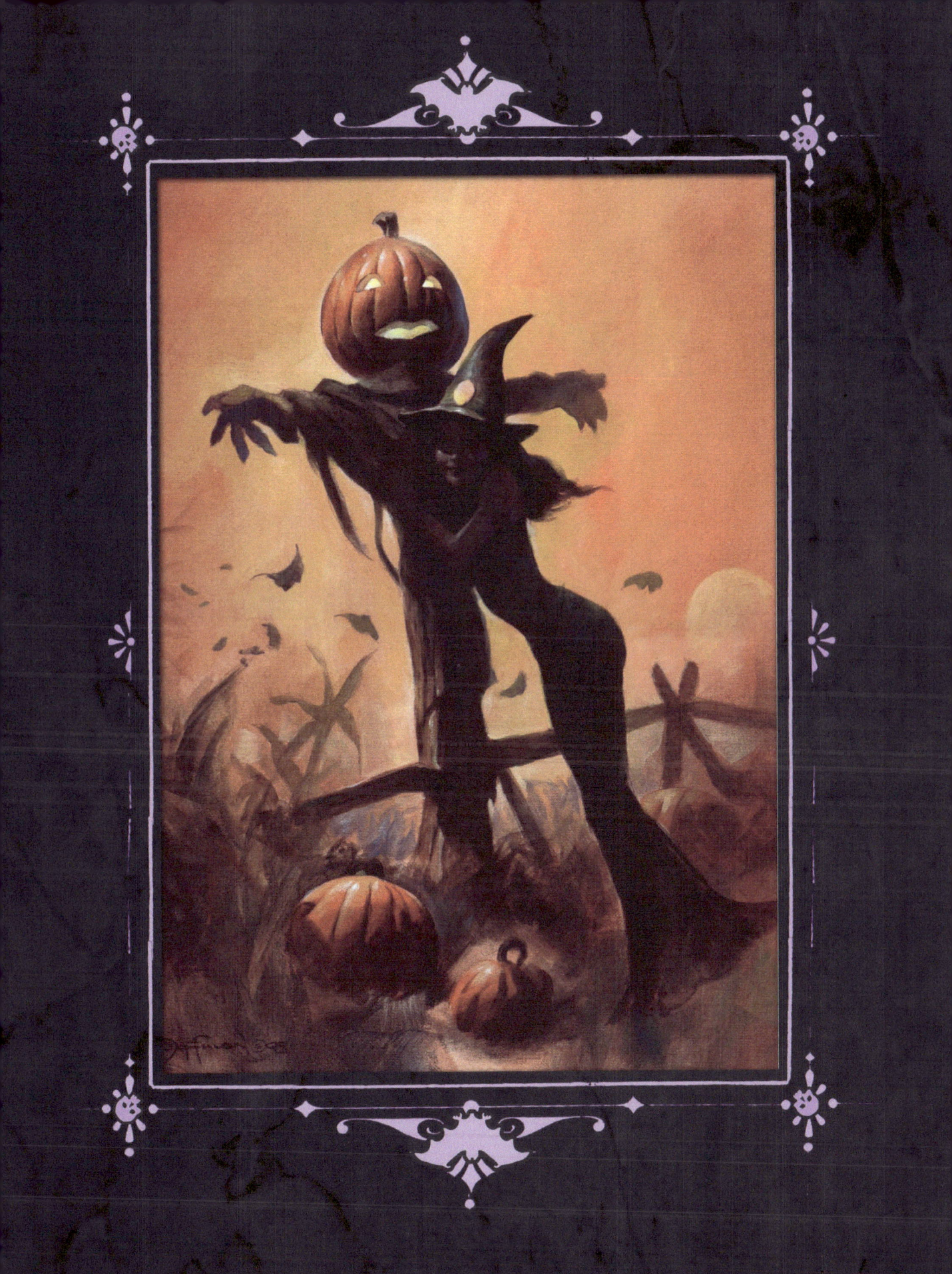

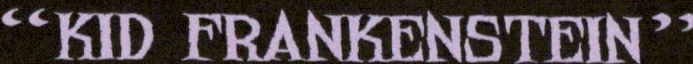

"KID FRANKENSTEIN"

NINE MONTHS PASSED
IN THE WINK OF AN EYE
HIS DEAR BELOVED
WAS EATING PICKLES
AND ICE CREAM
WHO'D HAVE THOUGHT
THAT IT COULD
END THIS WAY?
AND THE MONSTER
BUILT BY FRANKENSTEIN
WAS HEARD TO SAY:
'YOU GOT MY LOOKS
SO I KNOW YOU'RE MY SON,
AND A SQUARE HEAD
IS MUCH BETTER
THAN ROUND'

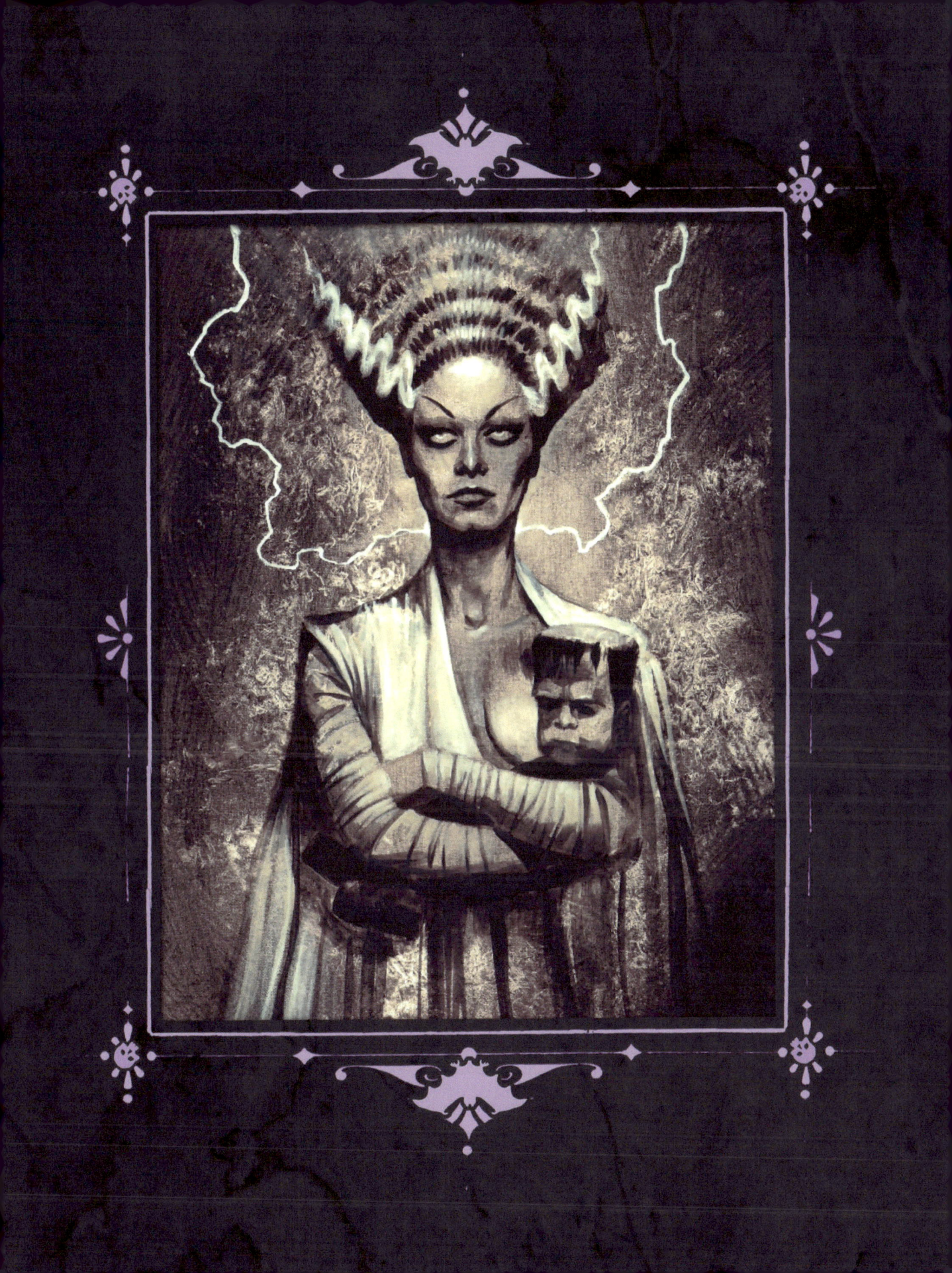

"HALLOWEEN HOOLIGANS"

THESE KIDS ARE BAD NEWS!
WITH POINTED SHOES
AND POINTED HAT
A WITCH LEADS
THE TROOP
'TO SPOOK'

CHASING BATS
AND BLACK CATS
THEY CAN ONLY BE STOPPED
BY THE SIGHT
OF SWEET SNACKS

JUST BE WARY
FOR THEIR TRICKS ARE
TROUBLES TO REPAIR!

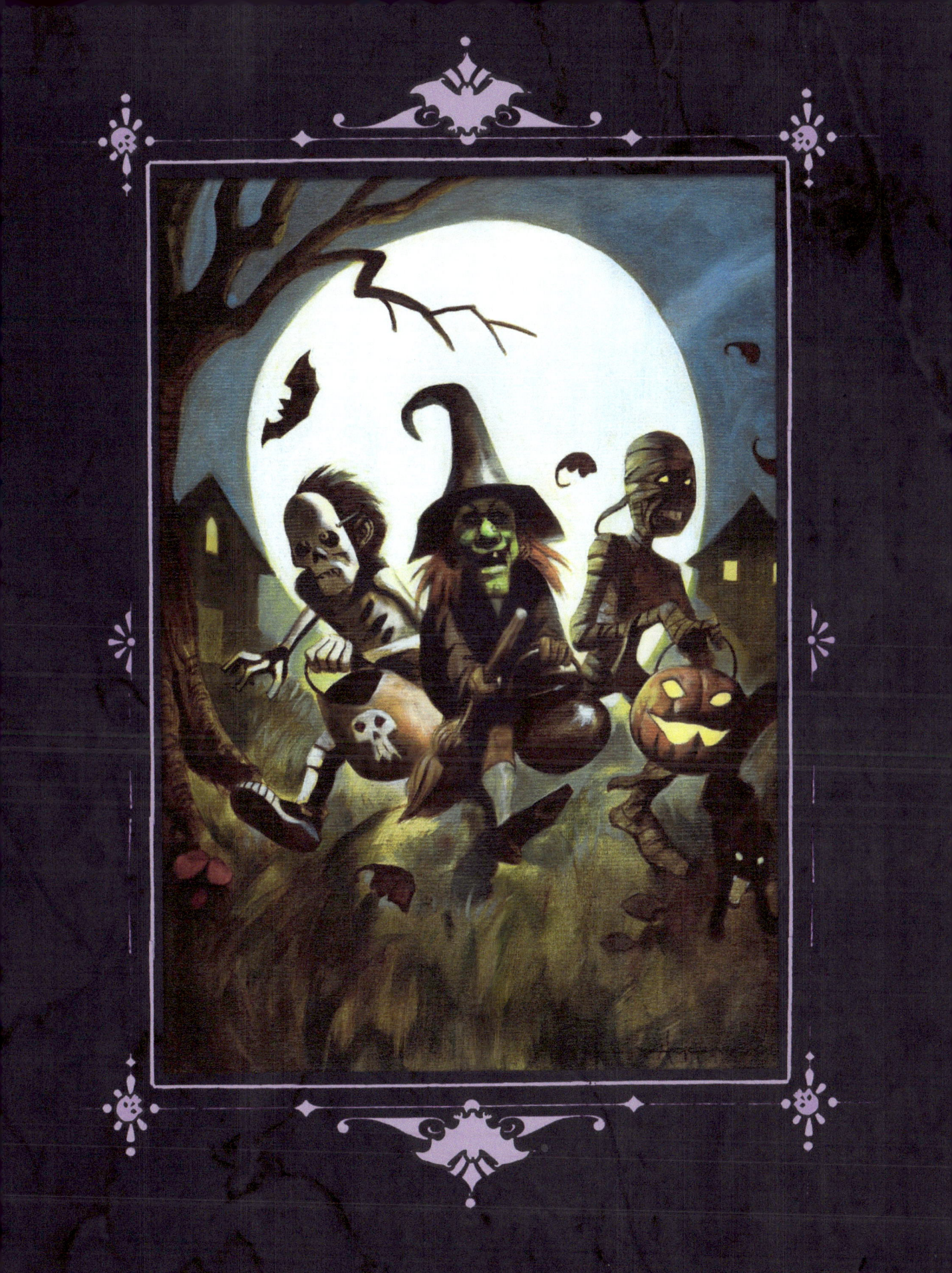

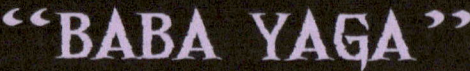

"BABA YAGA"

THE FAMOUS WITCH
OF RUSSIAN FOLKLORE
HAS GOTTEN A BAD RAP
BUT WE'LL SETTLE THE SCORE
WHILE WITCHCRAFTING PURISTS
GET ALL IN A FLAP
STILL SHE HOVERS IN AIR
IN PESTLE-TUB CONTRAPTION,
WITHOUT NARY A CARE
AS HER PAD
PERAMBULATES EVERYWHERE
WITH A CERTAIN SKINNY
CHICKEN-LEGGED GAIT
EASILY HOPPING THAT FENCE
MADE OF BONES
OF THE INGRATE

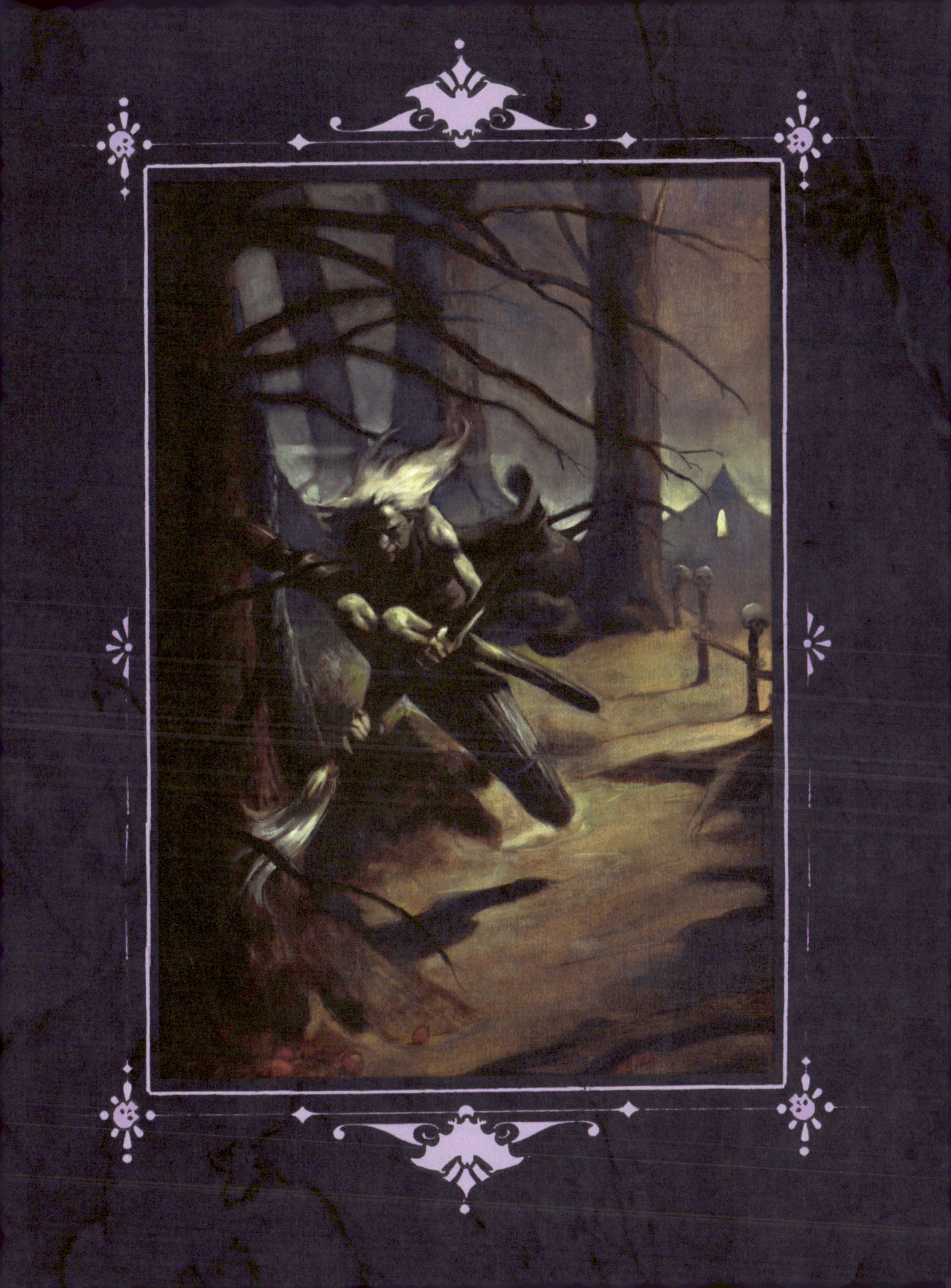

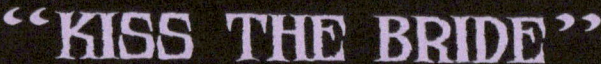

"KISS THE BRIDE"

WILD, WILD HAIR
WITH A SHEET AS A GOWN
SPITTIN' AT FRANKIE
WHEN THE SLAB COMES DOWN
EYES LIKE LIGHTNING
CRAZY ALL OF THE TIME
IF YOU THINK SHE'LL
DO THE DISHES
THEN YOU'RE OUT
OF YOUR MIND...

KISS THE BRIDE
OF FRANKENSTEIN
SHE SAYS 'GIVE ME THE
JUICE, IT'S LIKE LIGHTNING!'

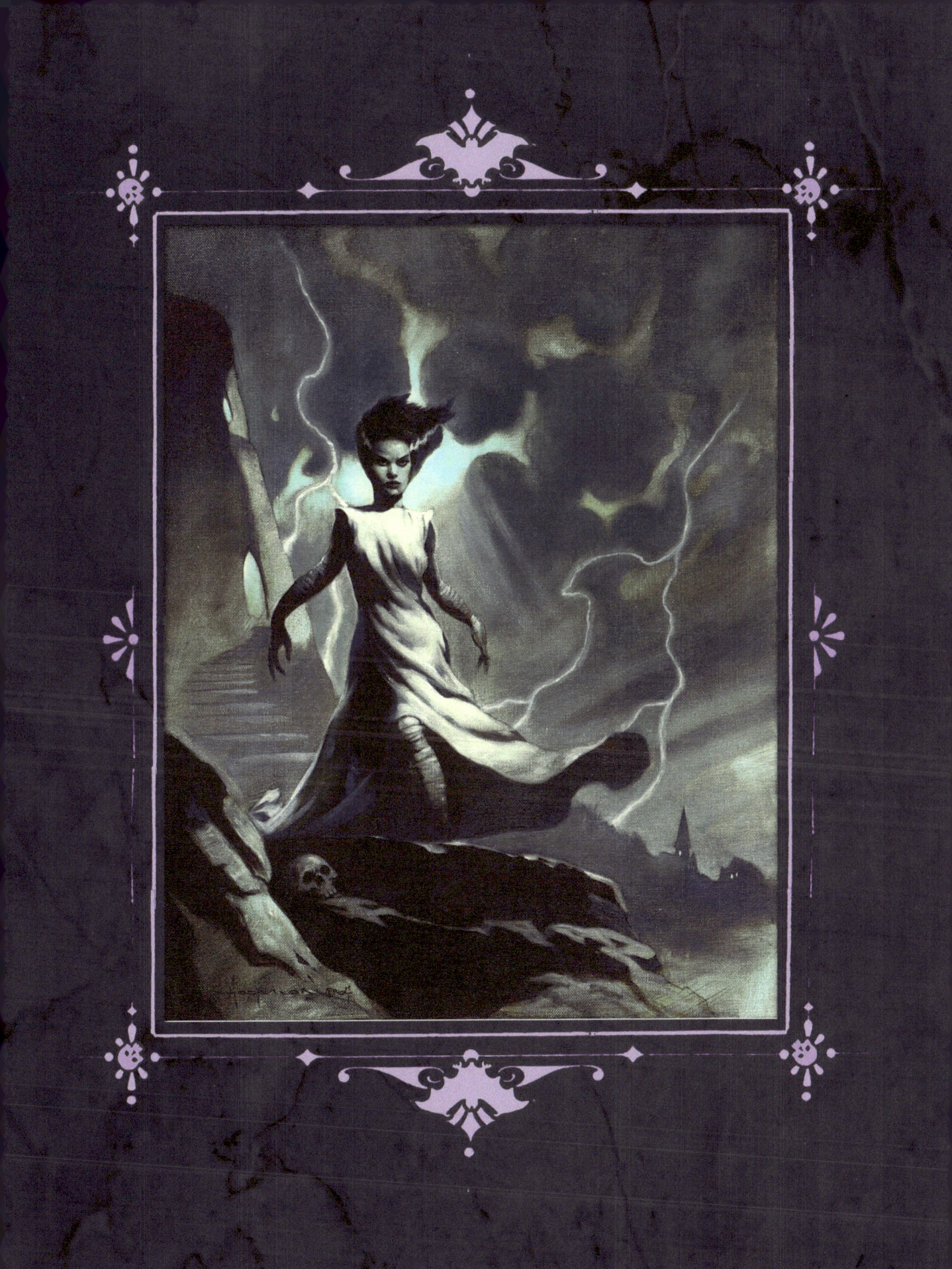

"THE DEMON"

HE'S NOT SO BAD
IN FACT HE'S SAD
WE ALL MAKE MISTAKES
AND POOR CHOICES
FOR PICKING A SIDE
IS LIKE A SWORD
OR A KNIFE
EACH ONE CAN SLICE
OFF A BIG HUNK OF YOU
AND THAT'S VERY TRUE
SO THE NEXT TIME
YOU LOOK DOWN
AT SOMEONE FROM
THE BAD SIDE OF TOWN
REMEMBER, MY FRIEND
IT COULD ALWAYS BE YOU.

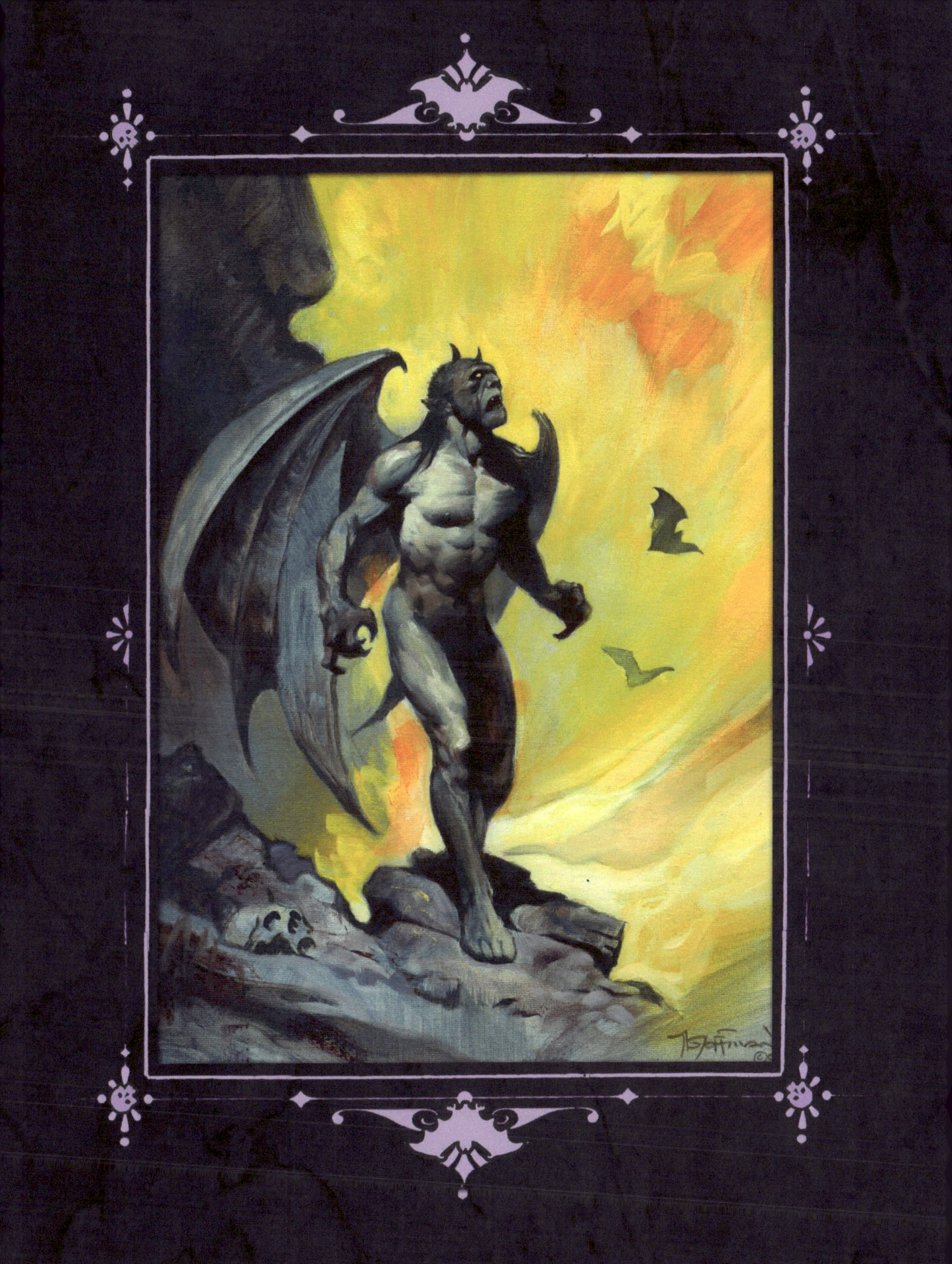

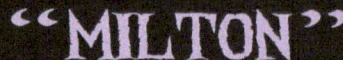

"MILTON"

THE SOUL
OF A CHILD
IN THE BODY
OF A MONSTER
FATHERED BY A MADMAN
WITH NO MOTHER
TO NURSE YA
BUT IN SPITE OF
YOUR STRENGTH
AND INCREDIBLE POWERS
YOU CARE NOT
TO RUN AMOK
YOU'D RATHER
PICK FLOWERS

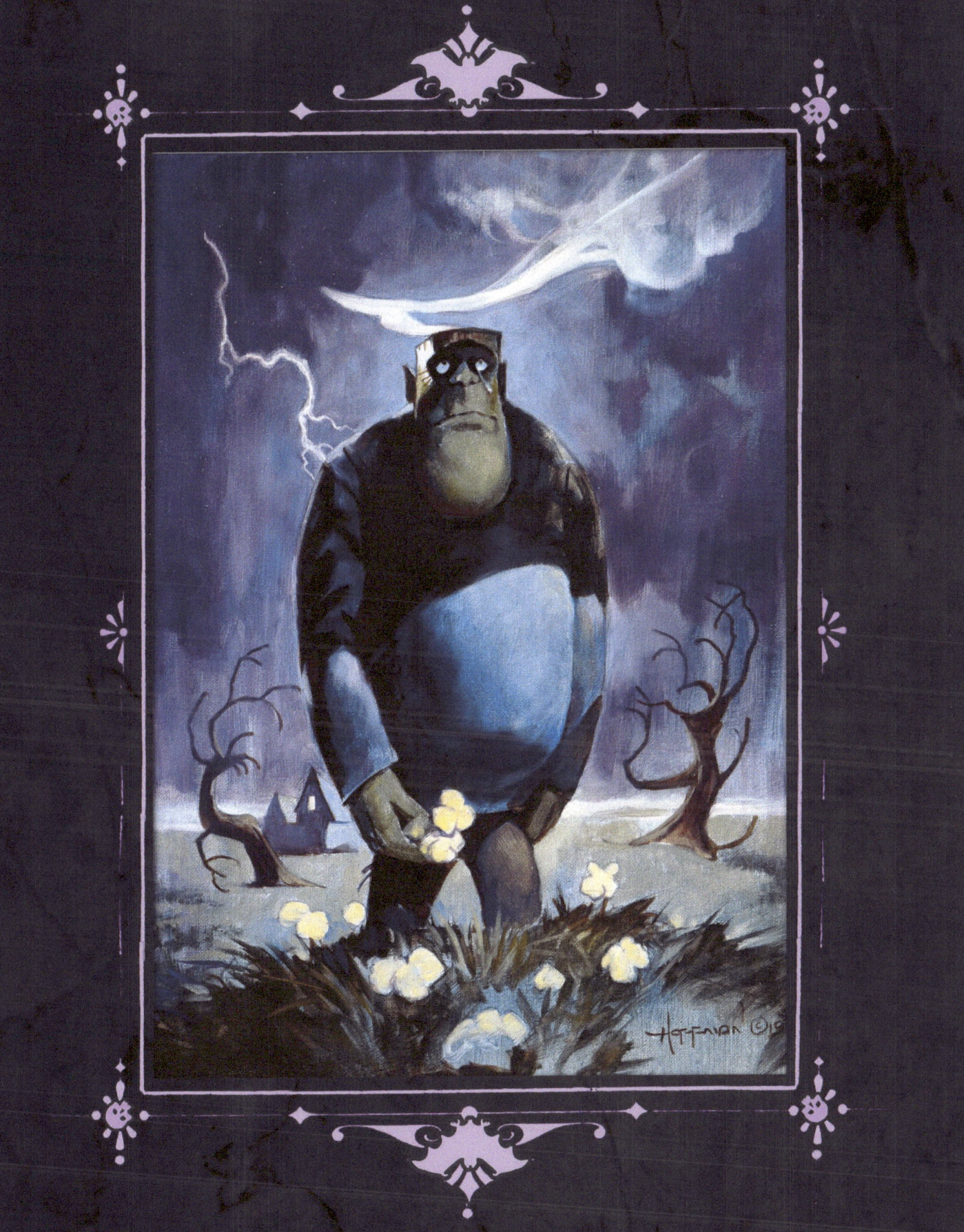

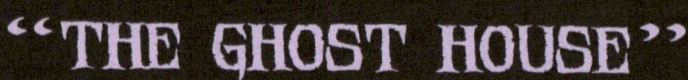

"THE GHOST HOUSE"

GHOSTS AND GOBLINS
ALL AROUND
DON'T BE AFRAID
IF YOU HEAR A SOUND

FOOTSTEPS RINGING
THROUGH EMPTY HALLS
VOICES SCREAM
AS DARKNESS FALLS

SKELETONS DANCE
QUITE CHEERILY
AROUND THE GRAVES
OF THE DEPARTED DEAR

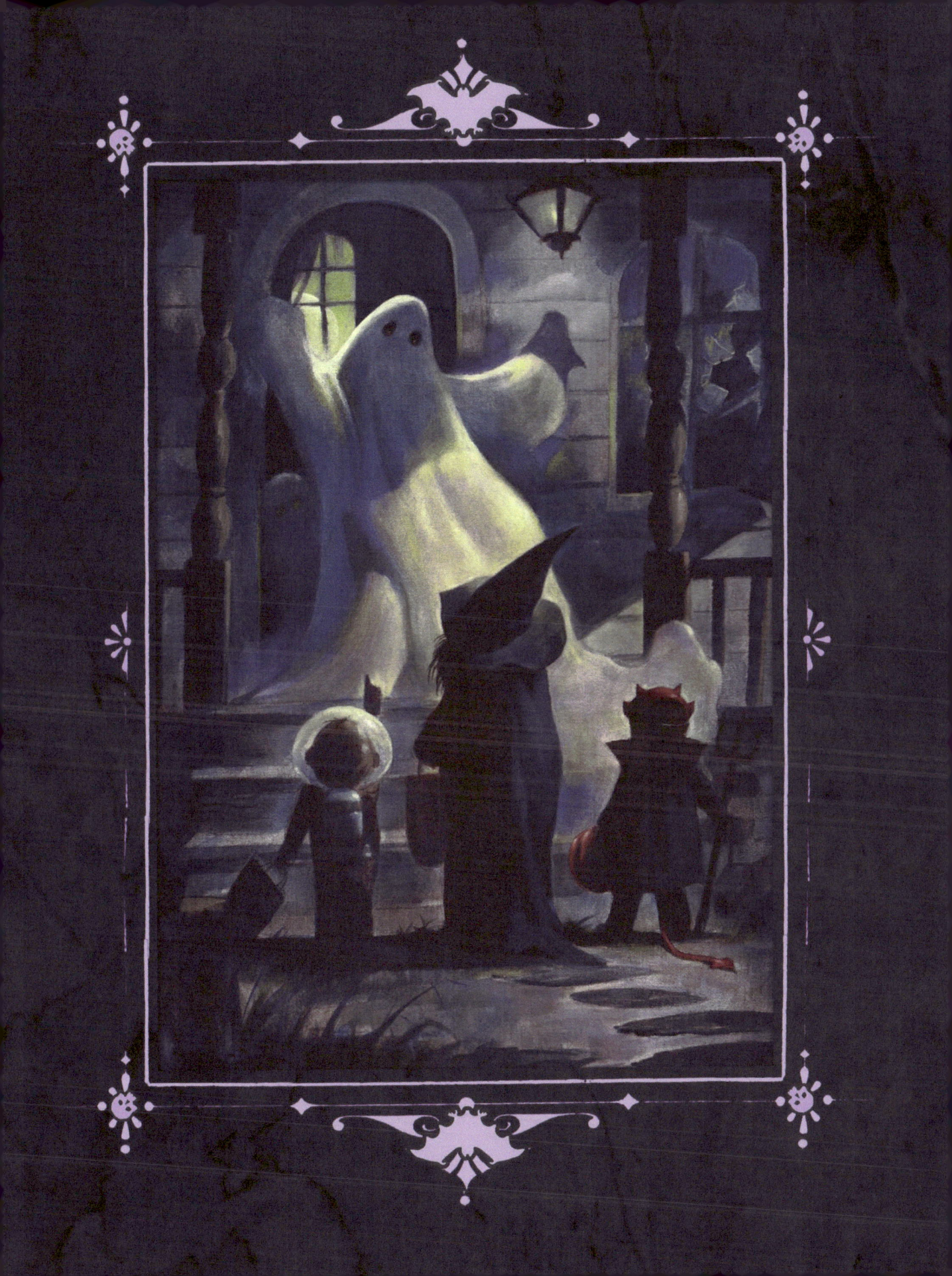

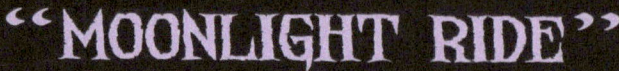

"MOONLIGHT RIDE"

O LOVELY WITCH
SWEET MOON FLOWER
ASTRIDE YOUR TRUSTY BROOM
IT'S GOOD FOR MORE
THAN JUST THE FLOOR
WHEN SWEEPING OUT A ROOM
THE COOL NIGHT AIR
CARESS YOUR HAIR
YOUR RAVEN TRESSES
ARE BLOWN ASUNDER
IF THAT BROOM COULD TALK
WHAT WOULD IT SAY?
WOULD IT COMPLAIN
OR REJOICE
I WONDER?

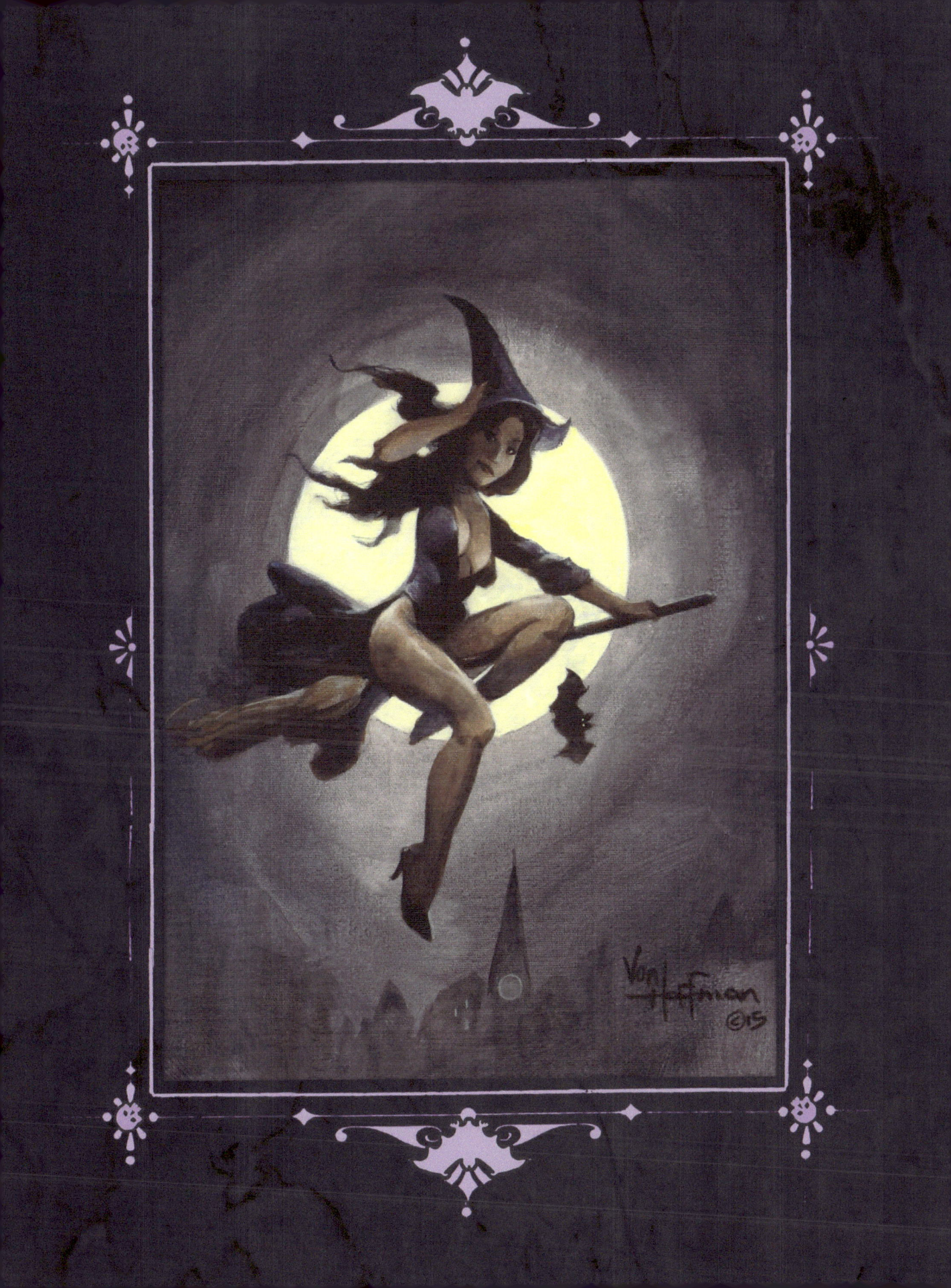

"MIDNIGHT MONSTER"

THREE LITTLE
TRICK-OR-TREATERS
ALL IN A ROW
TROMPING THROUGH
A GRAVEYARD
BETTER NOT BE SLOW!
YOU NEVER KNOW
WHAT'S FOLLOWING YOU
OR WHAT KIND OF THING
MAY LURK;
FOR IF YOU MEET
A MONSTER AT MIDNIGHT
YOU'LL KNOW HE'S
HARD AT WORK!

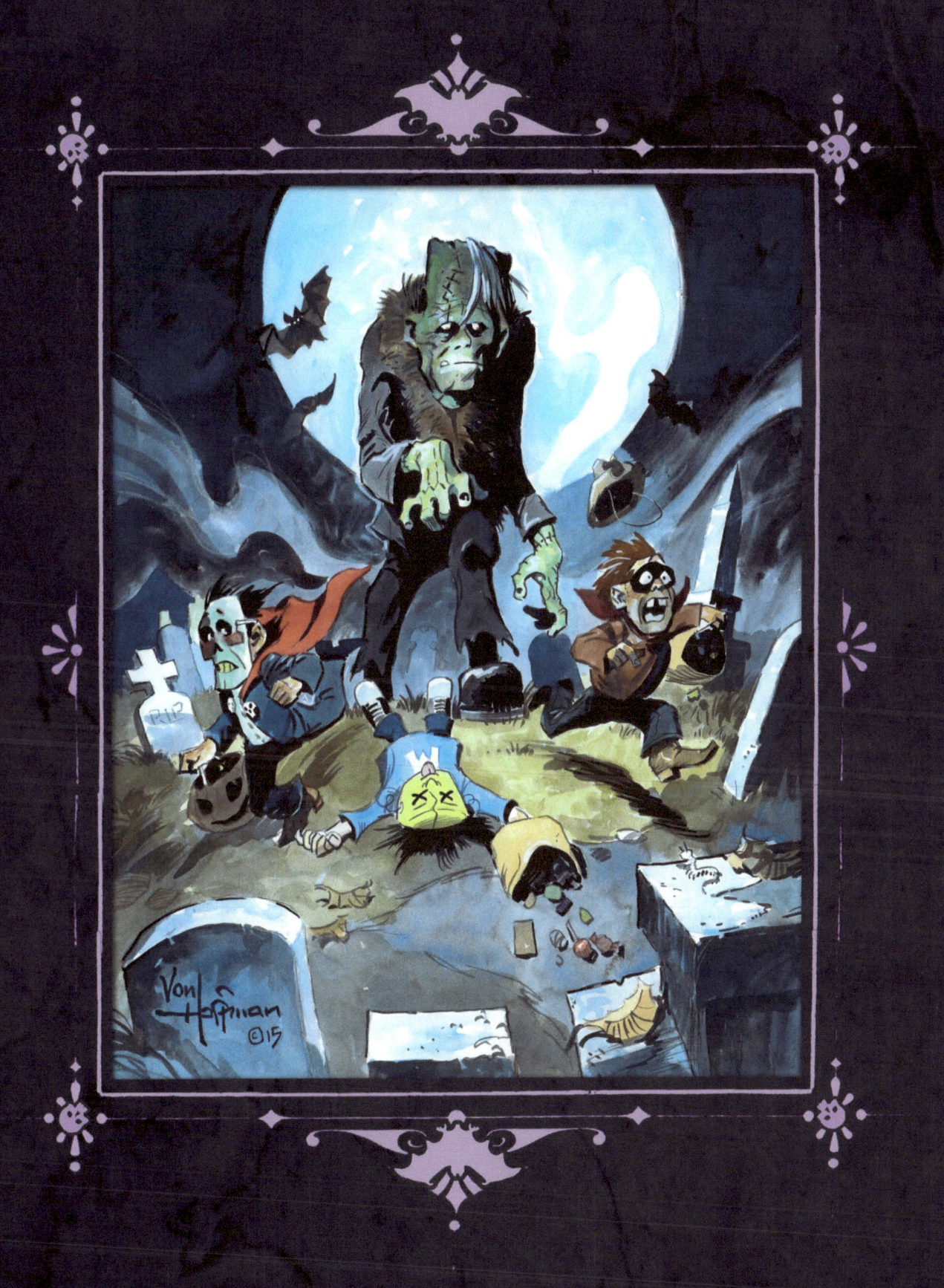

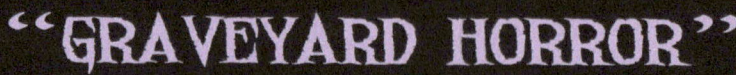

"GRAVEYARD HORROR"

THREE KIDS DRAGGIN'
BAGS OF CANDY AND JUNK
WALK THROUGH THE GRAVEYARD
NOW WHO WOULD HAVE THUNK?

THAT UP THERE
ON A GRAVESTONE
PUFFING A CIGAR
SAT DEAR DEAD OLD FREDERICK,
YOUR GREAT UNCLE, REMEMBER?

HE JUST POPPED OUT
TO SEE HOW YOU WERE
TO GIVE HIS BELOVED NEPHEW
AND HIS FRIENDS
A NICE LITTLE SCARE

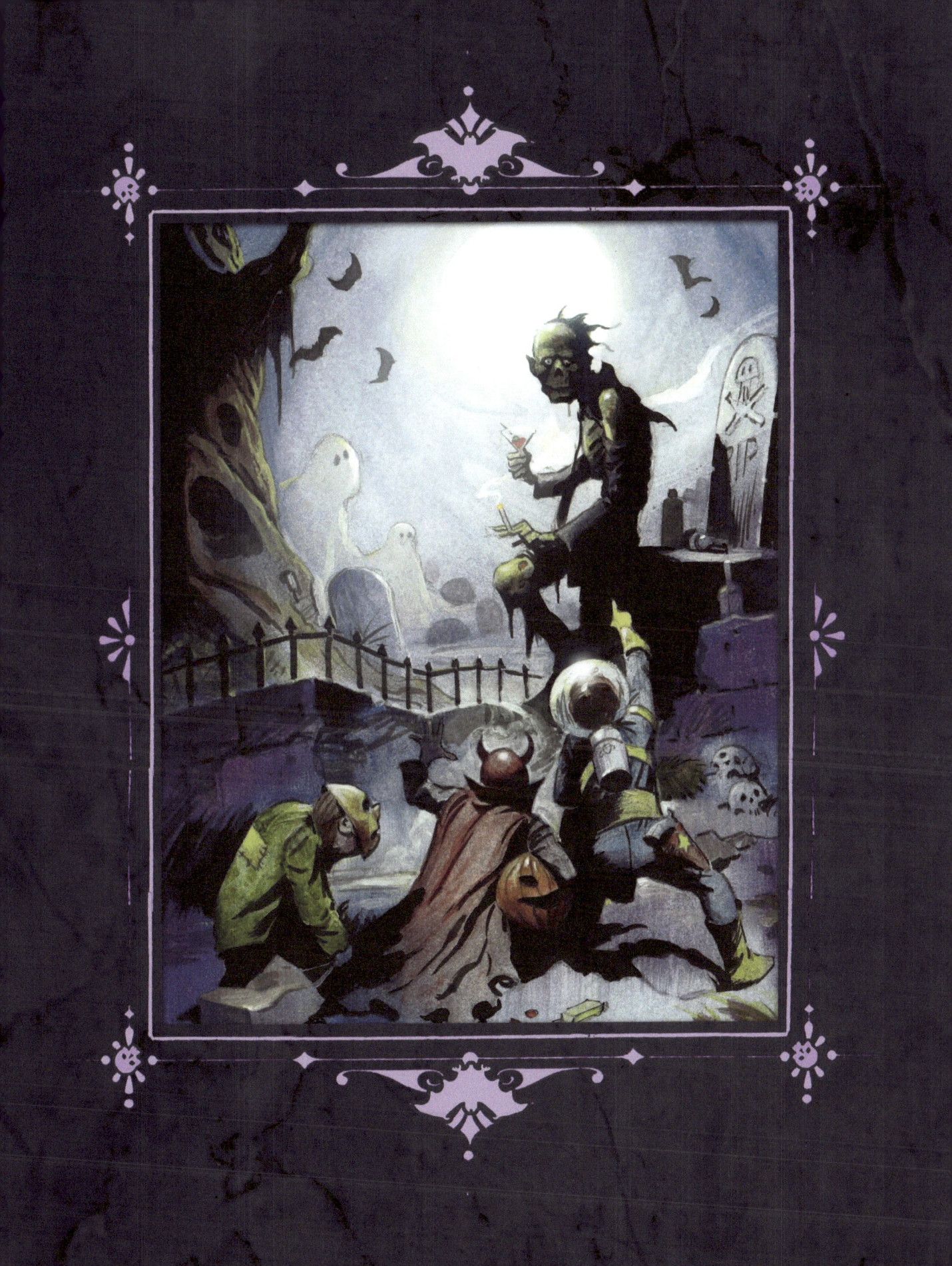

"HAUNTED HOUSE"

THE OLDEST OF
THREE YOUNG CHILDREN
ON ONE HALLOWEEN NIGHT
DECIDED THE OTHER TWO
COULD DO WITH A FRIGHT
'THERE'S NO SUCH THING
AS GHOSTS' ONE SAID
THE OTHER, 'I'M NOT
AFRAID OF THE DARK!'
BUT IN ANY CASE
THEY TOOK THEIR DOG
WHICH SOON BEGAN TO BARK
FOR GHOSTS WERE FLUTTERING
YET TWO WERE NOT SCARED
BUT THE BRAINS OF
THE OPERATION
WAS SUDDENLY NO-WHERE!

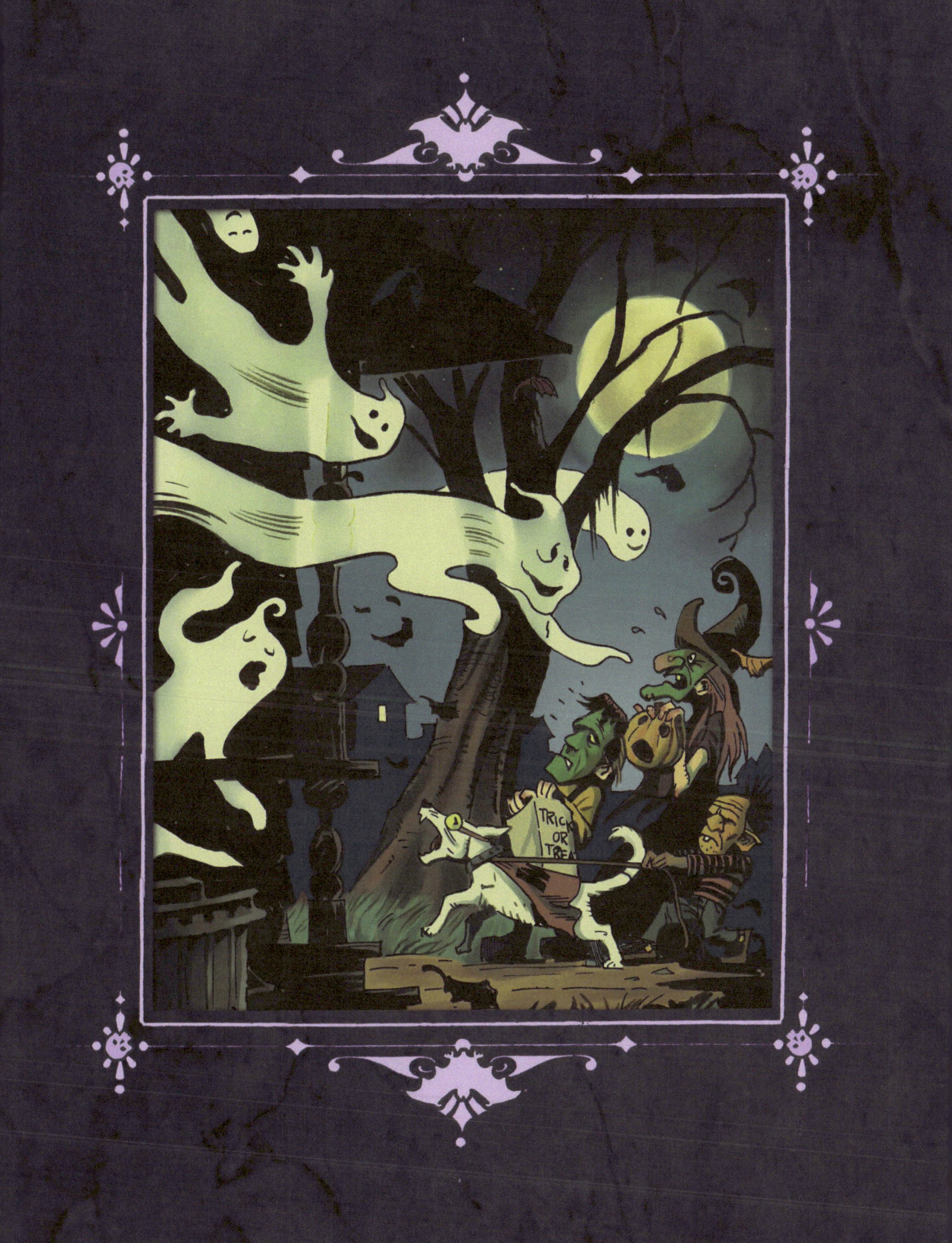

"SPOOKY GIRL"

OTHER KIDS
DON'T LIKE HER
SHE HAS NO HUMAN FRIENDS
BUT OTHERS LIKE GHOSTS,
GOBLINS AND CREATURES
FLOCK TO HER
FROM EVERYWHERE

IN THE FINAL ANALYSIS
IT'S NOT THE COMPANY
THAT YOU KEEP
STRANGE BEINGS
MAY TERRIFY YOU
INTO PARALYSIS
THEY'RE *HER* COMPANY,
YOU CREEP!

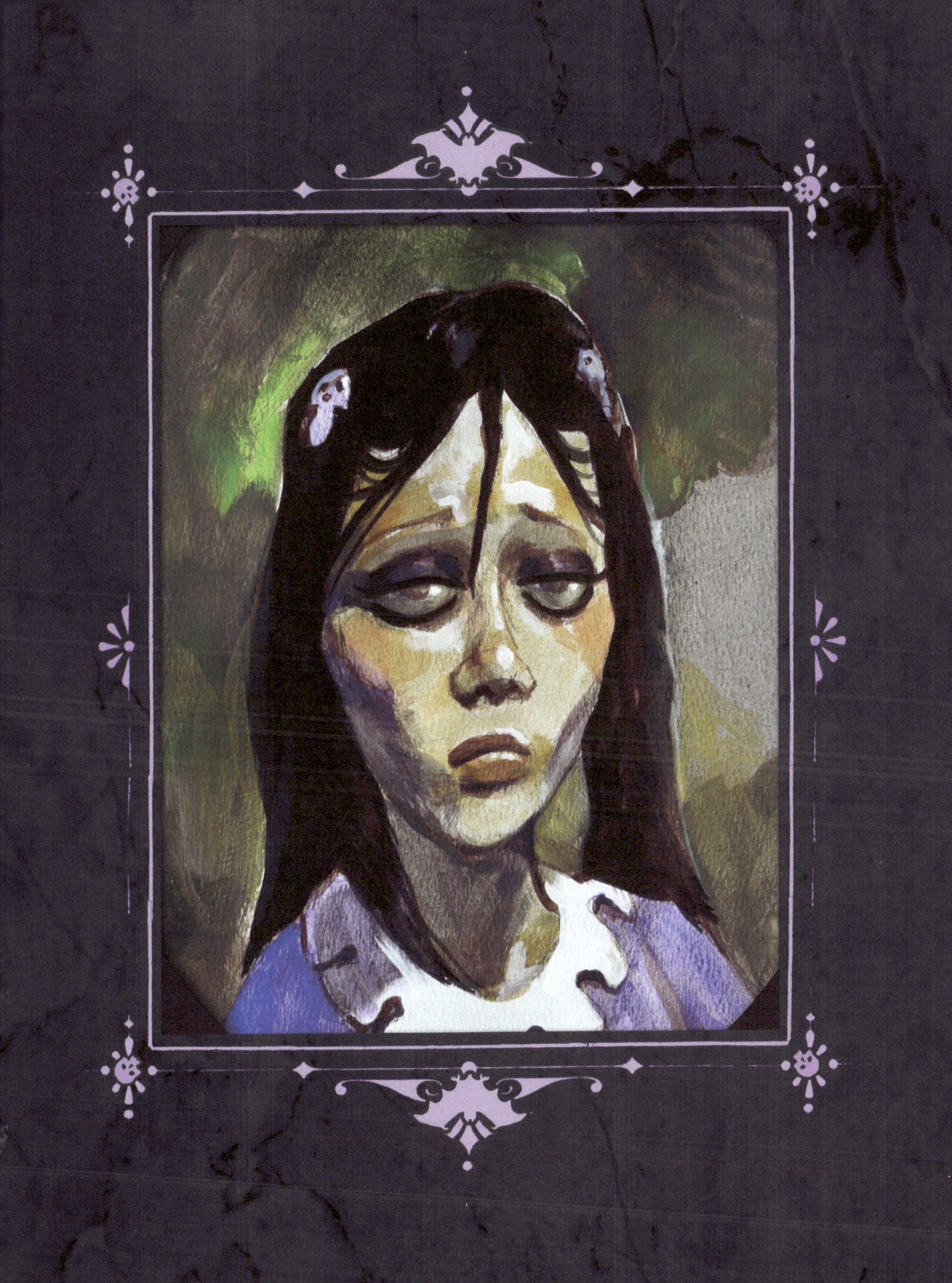

"MR. PUMPKINHEAD"

WHEN THE OCTOBER MOON
IS FULL IN THE SKY
AND LITTLE CHILDREN
ALL AROUND THE WORLD
DRESS UP AND THEN CRY
'TRICK OR TREAT!
TRICK OR TREAT!'
AT THE TOP OF THEIR LUNGS
IN PRECIOUS LITTLE TIME
MR. PUMPKINHEAD COMES
JUST TO TELL THEM
HE'S NOT TOO SCARED TO SAY
THAT THE 'TRICK' PART
OF HALLOWEEN
IS LIKE A KNIFE
THAT CUTS BOTH WAYS

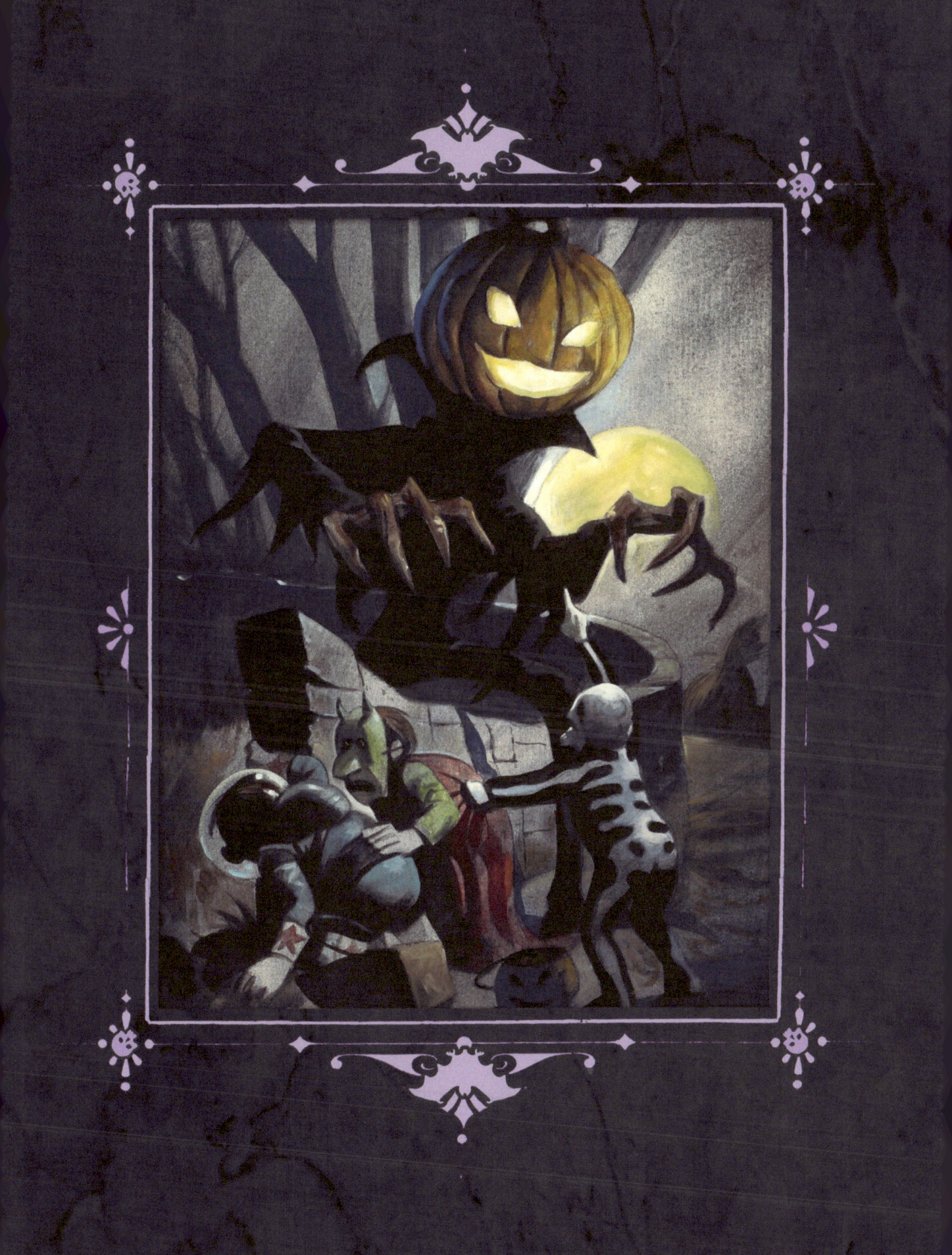

"FRANKENSTEIN"

ONCE UPON AS TIME
IN A GREAT BIG CASTLE
A MAN AND A MONSTER
GOT INTO A HASSLE

THE MONSTER WAS LONELY
BECAUSE HE WANTED A MATE
THE MAD DOCTOR SAID
'BOY, YOU'LL
HAVE TO WAIT'

THE MONSTER SAID
'COME ON, DOCTOR
FRANKENSTEIN,
BUILD A WOMAN
AND MAKE HER MINE'

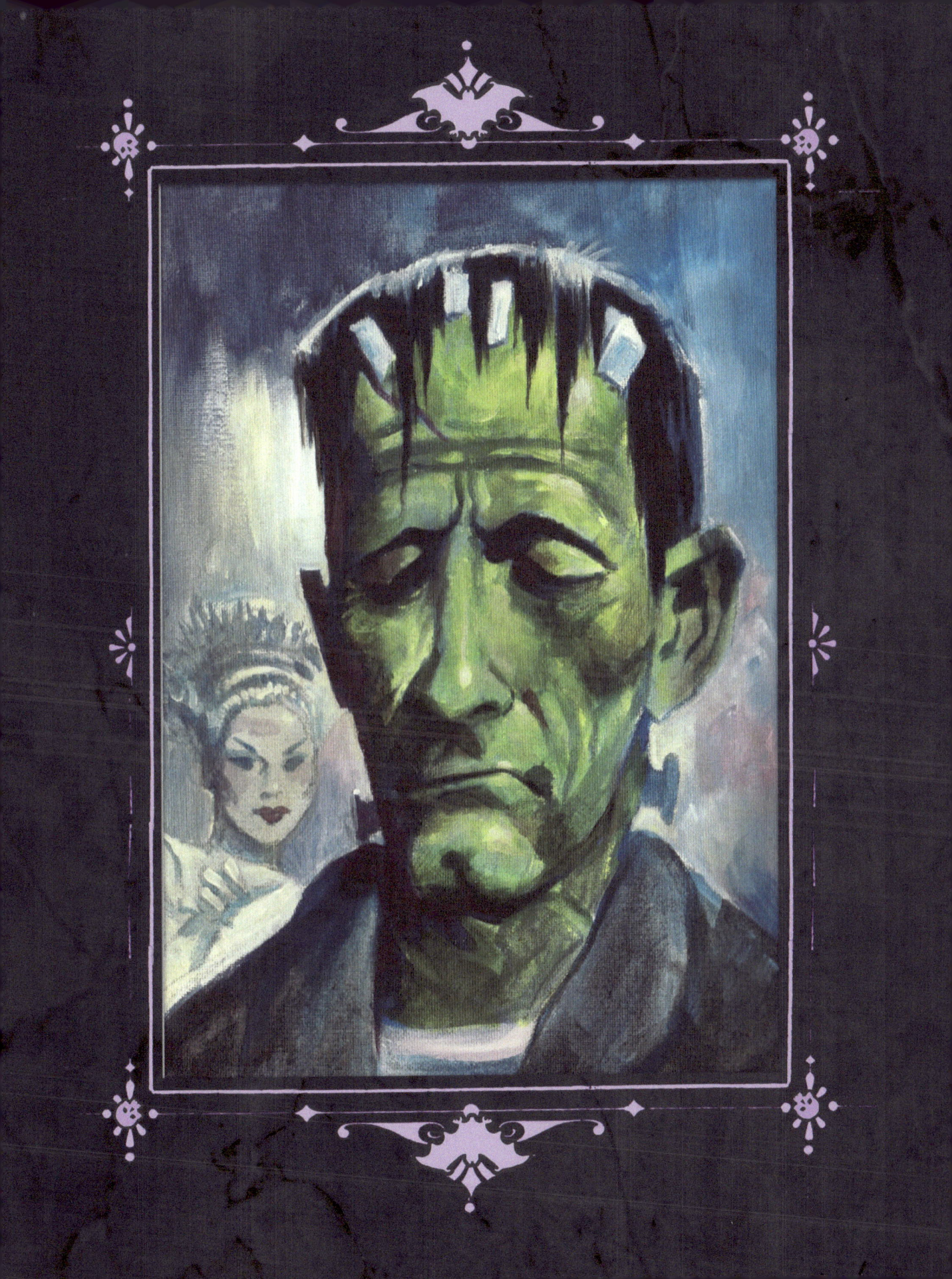

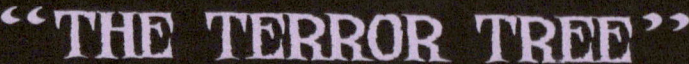

"THE TERROR TREE"

JUST A GANG OF KIDS
UP TO NO GOOD
STOMPING AROUND
BY THE EDGE OF THE WOOD
ON HALLOWEEN NIGHT
WHEN THE MOON RIDES SO HIGH
ALL THE WHILE
THEY ARE SEEN
BY THE SPIRITS
OF THE TREES
THEY WILL CRY 'WHY DO I FEEL
AS IF WE'RE BEING WATCHED?'
BUT DON'T TURN TO SEE
FOR THOSE HORRIBLE BRANCHES
MAY CLUTCH AND CATCH
IF YOU SCREAM...

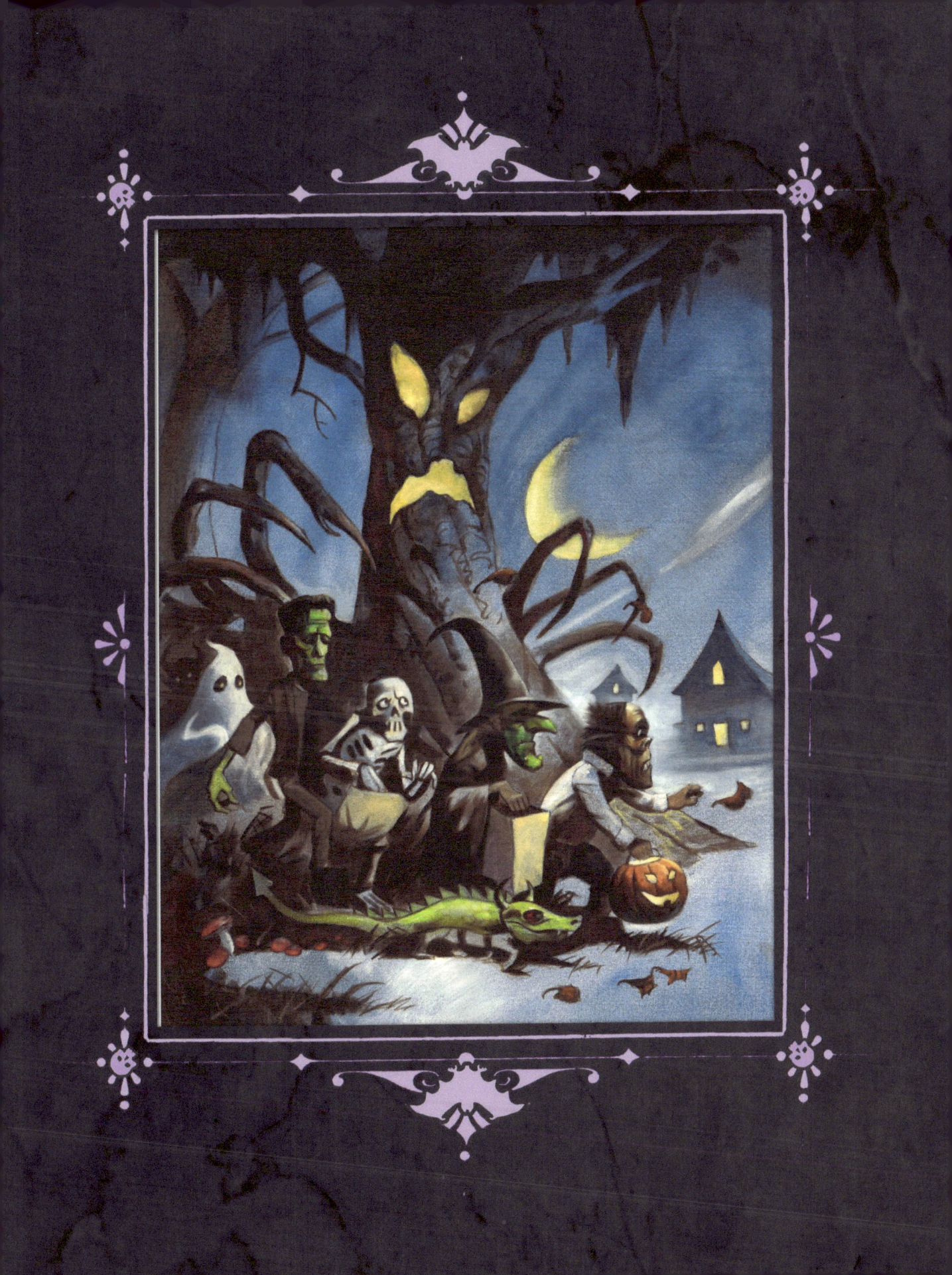

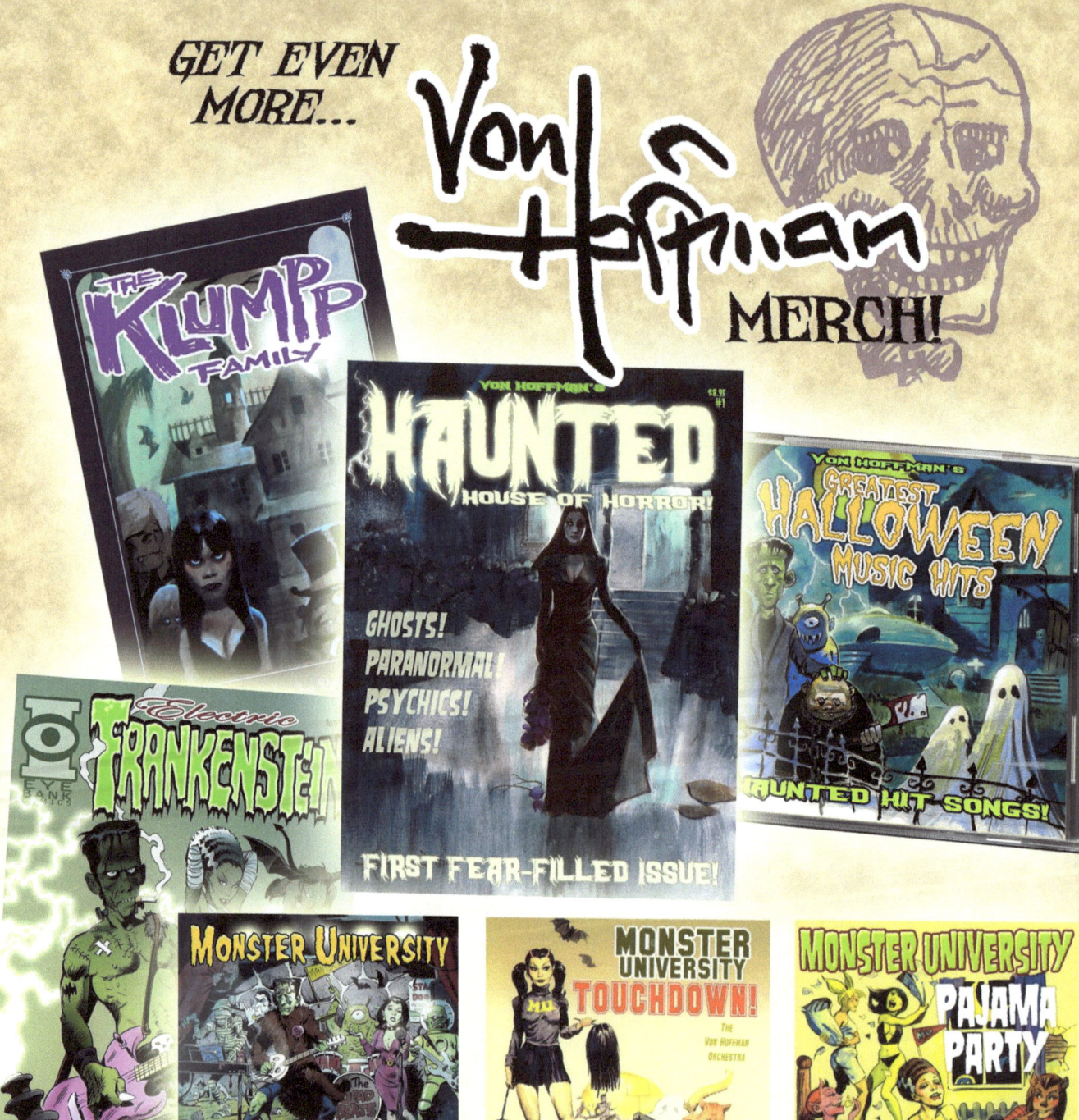